Logging Machines in the Forest

Logging
Machines

Illustrated with photographs

in the Forest

Janet Chiefari

Dodd, Mead & Company
New York

*I gratefully acknowledge the logger who inspired,
guided, and supported this project, Mr. John Basolt.*

Library of Congress Cataloging in Publication Data

Chiefari, Janet.
    Logging machines in the forest.

    Includes index.
    Summary: Describes the machines used to harvest trees
in the logging industry, including the saws and felling
shears that cut down and trim the trees, the skidders
that move the logs from the forest to the landing site,
and the loaders that place them onto the trucks for
hauling.
    1. Lumbering—Machinery—Juvenile literature.
[1. Lumber and lumbering—Machinery]   I. Title.
SD388.C487   1985   634.9′82′028   84-21062
ISBN 0-396-08564-4

PICTURE CREDITS

Clark Michigan Company, 38; Caterpillar Tractor Co., 12, 14, 15, 20, 26, 28, 42, 44; John Deere & Company, 10, 13, 17, 29, 30, 32, 36, 43, 56; FESCO, 59; Forrex, Inc., 31; Gafner Machine, Inc., 40; Great Lakes Tractors, 47; Harnischfeger Corporation, 48, 49; Morbark Industries, Inc., 21, 23, 24, 25, 27, 52, 53, 54, 55; Omark Industries, endpapers, 45, 46, 50; Roy Teal, 18, 19, 34; Tree Farmer Equipment Co., Inc., 35, 39; R. A. Whitfield Manfacturing Co., 57, 58.

Timber, the crop of the forest, is one of our greatest natural resources. The business of felling trees, cutting them into logs and transporting the logs from forest to market is called "timber harvesting" or "logging."

Logging was one of the first industries in America. To clear land for farms and towns, many trees were cut down. They were taken to sawmills to be sawed into lumber—boards used for building houses, barns, and churches. Wood was used to make furniture, crates, and many other items. Wood was also the fuel burned to heat homes.

Logging is a leading industry today, because people continue to have a great need for things made from wood. With 500 million acres of forest which can be logged, the United States is one of the world's largest timber-harvesting countries.

How are all these trees harvested? Would you expect to see huge, powerful machines in the forest? They are there, making logging faster, easier, and more efficient than ever before.

When a forest area has been selected for logging, a *landing* is prepared. This is a place where the logs will be brought to be sorted, stacked, and then loaded onto trucks.

Diesel-powered tractors—on wheels or on tracks—clear this site. The tractors come equipped with different types of front blades which can be raised and lowered. These mighty machines push over small trees, and then move trees and brush to clear a space for the landing.

Also part of preparing the forest for logging is the construction of roads and trails. These will take men and machines to the trees that are to be cut. Logs will be hauled back to the landing over the roads.

Excavators and bulldozers handle the work of building roads. The excavator's hydraulic bucket scoops up earth and moves it. Bulldozers are track-type tractors with steel blades to push aside earth and underbrush.

The motor grader flattens and smooths the roads. This type of grader has power steering to each wheel—called all-wheel drive. The logger can easily move the 125-horsepower machine over steep, narrow, winding logging roads.

Once the roads are built, the motor grader is used to keep the road surfaces in good condition.

The machine a logger uses to fell, or cut down, trees will depend on the floor or ground of the forest, and the size and number of trees to be harvested. He uses the machine that will cause the least possible damage to the forest.

The logger often chooses a chain saw to do his job. The saw has a gasoline motor. It has a chain with a sharp cutting edge that moves around a stationary center bar.

With a chain saw, an experienced logger can fell the largest trees and drop them where they will not damage other trees. A wedge-shaped notch is made on one side, and removed. From the opposite side, another cut is sawed deep into the tree. When the tree begins to fall forward, the notch determines the direction. It drops to the forest floor exactly where the logger planned for it to go.

Some loggers use tractors equipped with a *felling shear* or a *felling saw* to cut down trees.

Like giant scissors, the hydraulically operated felling shear quickly snips through a tree 20 to 30 inches in diameter, and directs it to fall away from the tractor at a certain angle.

A felling shear or a felling saw can be attached to many kinds of tractors. Here is a felling saw called a grapple saw, fastened to the hydraulic boom of a tractor.

The grapple is like a hand that holds the tree and then lays it down on the ground when it has been sawed through.

After cutting down the tree, the grapple saw can be used to "buck" the tree. "Bucking" means sawing the tree into log lengths which will be easier to haul. The length of the logs will depend on what they are to be used for.

Several hundred trees an hour can be felled with a *feller buncher*. This is another kind of attachment that is mounted on the front of a tractor.

Feller bunchers come in different sizes. One with a large felling shear can handle trees up to 20 inches in diameter.

The feller buncher can cut one tree, then hold it while it cuts another. It cuts, holds, and then carries several small-diameter trees, or one large tree. It stacks the cut trees in neat piles, or bunches, ready to be hauled to the landing.

This feller buncher, mounted on a tractor, has a felling shear. It carries several cut trees at one time.

22

The felling shear cuts the tree close to the ground and leaves a depression or dent in the stump. Water will collect in this and help decay the stump. This will add nutrients to the soil and give room for new trees to grow.

This machine swings around on its base like a swivel chair. A feller buncher is attached to the hydraulic boom. Standing in one place, it can turn, and reach out as far as 29 feet to fell trees in a large circle around it.

A tractor with a feller buncher attached must move from tree to tree. This swing-type felling machine does not have to move around so much.

Wood for lumber, furniture, or floors comes from the trunks of big trees. Therefore, once a tree is on the ground, the top and limbs are trimmed off. This is done with a chain saw or by a machine called a *delimber*.

This John Deere 743A Tree-Harvester can run two to four trees per minute through its delimber.

A feller buncher on the Tree-Harvester fells the tree, then feeds it into the delimber. Big rolls, covered with spikes, grab the tree and pull it through the delimbing knives. They cut off all the limbs and the top.

Here the 743A has a grapple instead of a feller buncher. It picks up the trees, feeds them through the delimber, and then stacks the logs.

This mini-tractor is used to thin out small trees up to 10 inches in diameter. In southern pine forests, it can fell, delimb, buck, and stack over 100 trees an hour.

The felling shear cuts the tree and then turns it so that the tree is parallel to the ground. Two spiked rolls move it through delimbing knives at the high speed of 4.3 feet per second.

Because of its usefulness, the *skidder* is the machine most often seen in logging operations across the United States. The skidder has all-wheel drive. Its main job is to move the logs from the forest to the landing.

With the logs fastened behind, it drags—skids—them over rugged, uneven ground. Its large wheels, set wide apart, allow the skidder to get up over rocks and tree stumps.

This skidder has huge, oversized tires to give it "flotation"—to keep the machine from sinking into the ground by spreading its weight over a wider area. Thus, there is less damage to the soil and to the roots of trees.

There are two kinds of skidders—cable and grapple. This is a cable model. Loggers wrap a steel cable or wire rope, called a "choker," around the butt or large end of a giant log. A winch pulls it up close to the back of the machine. One end of the log drags on the ground in skidding.

A cable skidder can get hard-to-reach logs. It can pull
them out from behind stumps and rocks, and snake them
between trees and over winding trails.

31

The grapple skidder has a hydraulic grabbing claw called a grapple. It can rotate, or turn, and grab logs from any angle. Where logs are prebunched and easy to get at, this method is faster and safer than cable skidding because no one has to set wire chokers.

As the grapple skidder hauls the logs, they bump and move around. The grapple automatically squeezes more tightly to hold the logs.

A front blade is standard equipment on a skidder. It can be used for clearing the landing, building roads and skid trails, and for decking—piling up—logs.

This skidder is decking logs. It has tire chains on for increased traction.

The *forwarder* is another machine that brings logs out of
the forest. It has a loader which the logger uses to fill its
carrier with logs. In forwarding, the entire log is carried
off the ground, not dragged, as in skidding.

After logs reach the landing, they must be sorted and stacked according to their grade or value, and what kind of wood. This will determine what the logs will be used for and where they will be shipped.

Logs are loaded onto trucks by machines called *loaders*. Some log loaders have extended-reach "arms" and a rotating grapple. This kind is ideal for loading shortwood—wood that has been sawed into short lengths. Trucks or railroad cars will haul the shortwood to paper mills where it will be made into paper products such as writing paper, newspaper, and cardboard.

Some hardwoods, like cherry, maple, and oak, will be taken to furniture manufacturers. Some will go to mills to be made into railroad ties, fence posts, and telephone poles.

The huge, heavy logs are handled by loaders of different types. The four-wheel-drive loaders come equipped with the logger's choice of grapples or log forks.

Softwoods, such as these giant pine logs, will be taken to sawmills to be sawed into lumber for the building industry.

This is a track-type loader. It can lift 8,600 pounds with its log fork. Log forks are like two long arms that go under the logs, with a top clamp that closes over the logs to hold them firmly in place.

This giant Caterpillar log loader can carry and load up to 58,000 pounds of timber at one time with its huge forks. It has four speeds forward and four reverse, and a 375-horsepower engine.

A knuckleboom hydraulic loader can be mounted on a logging truck or trailer. The knuckleboom, like an arm, reaches out and clamps onto the logs with its grapple. Bending in at the elbow, or "knuckle," it swings the logs into the truck.

Logging trucks and trailers must be superstrong. The rig opposite has a self-loader at the back of its truck. The truck pulls a trailer called a pup trailer. It is known as a "dog-and-pup" rig.

The truck above has a semi-trailer and a pup trailer. They are ready to be loaded with shortwood. With 32 wheels and 55 feet in length, this rig can haul over 150,000 pounds.

This huge crane, called a portal crane, looks more like a bridge than a logging machine. But it can do the work of two or three log loaders and requires less fuel. The crane can stack logs 55 feet high.

The operator rides in a cab which moves back and forth with the crane on railway-type tracks. The monstrous grapples can empty a truck in one bite.

This portal crane lifts logs that have been moved by water to a central gathering place.

This powerful self-propelled loader is working with the *yarder* at left. It is part of the yarding system at a logging operation in Oregon.

"Yarding" is moving logs by means of cables. Chokers are set around the log. Then the yarder's diesel-driven winch reels the log up the hill.

Yarding is used in forest areas that are too steep or too rough for skidders and forwarders.

47

Sometimes trees are cut into chips or small pieces before they are shipped. This is done with a machine called a *whole tree chipper*. It also makes chips from the tops and limbs of trees that have been trimmed off.

The whole tree chipper has a hydraulic boom which feeds the trees or limbs into the chipper. It blows the chips into a 40-foot-long van, filling it in less than ten minutes. Chips are used to supply heat and electricity for many industries.

The whole tree chipper is useful for disposing of "junk" wood from the forest. Junk wood is trees that are dead or dying, diseased, or overcrowded. Removing it thins out the forest. Young, healthy trees are given room to grow strong and straight for future harvesting. Wood chips can be made from trees not good enough for board lumber.

If a logger is harvesting wood chips for the paper market, chips are put through a special screening system. High-quality chips needed for paper are separated from poorer-quality chips used for fuels.

This screening machine is blowing the two kinds of chips into separate vans at the rate of 150 tons per hour.

Wood chips are transported to large storage facilities where the trailers are emptied by a *chip van dump*. In just a few minutes, a 40-foot van can be dumped, lowered, hooked up to the truck again, and on its way back to the landing site for another load.

Most farmers harvest yearly crops, but trees may take 50 years or more before they are ready to be harvested. Therefore, loggers must plan for the future.

Maintaining healthy, productive forests can be done through conservation—the careful and responsible use of our present forests—and by reforestation—the planting of new trees to replace the ones taken.

Getting fields that have been logged ready for replanting is done by machines. They beat and grind the brush and roots and break up large clumps of dirt.

After the earth is leveled and smoothed, it is ready for planting the seedlings—trees under three feet in height that have been grown from seeds in large tree nurseries.

Machines also help plant the seedlings. Here a tractor pulls two tree planters.

A blade under the planter breaks open the soil. Then the man places a seedling into the planting "finger"—the bar sticking out from the chain in front of him. The finger takes the seedling to the opened ground and plants it. Two small wheels pack the soil around the tiny tree.

This tree planter can plant 2,000 seedlings in an hour because it automatically ejects them into the soil.

Our forests should always be able to supply our need for timber products if we use them wisely and see that new trees replace the ones taken out in logging operations.

Glossary

BUCKING — Sawing tree into log lengths.

BUNCH — To gather logs into small piles for hauling.

CABLE — Wire rope.

CHAIN SAW — Hand-held machine used to fell trees.

CHIP VAN DUMP — Hydraulic device used to lift and empty a van.

CHOCKER — Short length of cable wrapped around log to be skidded or yarded.

DECKING — Piling logs.

DELIMBING — Cutting off limbs and tops of trees.

FELLER BUNCHER — Tractor- or boom-mounted machine used to cut down, carry, and bunch trees.

FELLING — Cutting down a tree.

FELLING SAW OR SHEAR — Tractor- or boom-mounted machine used to fell trees.

FORWARDING — Entire tree carried off the ground to the landing.

GRAPPLE — Clawlike attachment used to pick up and hold logs and trees.

HYDRAULIC — Power from use of pressure from a quantity of water or other fluid being forced through a small opening.

KNUCKLEBOOM — An armlike machine attachment.

LANDING — Place where logs are brought to be sorted, stacked, and loaded.

LOADER — Machine used to load logs into a carrier.

LOG — Section of tree trunk suitable for lumber or other wood product.

LOGGER — One working in the production of logs.

LOGGING — The business of felling trees, cutting them into logs, and transporting them from forest to market.

LUMBER — Timber sawed into boards for use in building.

MOTOR GRADER — Machine used to level and smooth logging roads.

SKIDDER — Machine used to drag logs; can be cable skidder or grapple skidder.

SKIDDING — Pulling or dragging logs or trees from stump to landing.

STUMP — Part of tree and roots left in ground after felling.

TIMBER — The crop of the forest: trees, wood.

TIMBER HARVESTING — Logging.

WHOLE TREE CHIPPER — Machine used to cut trees into small pieces or chips.

WINCH — Machine having one or more barrels or drums on which to coil a cable; used for hauling logs.

YARDING — Moving logs by means of cables.

Index